C000174920

I Was Writing This Diary
For You, Sasha

I Was Writing This Diary For You, Sasha

By
Hana Pravda

Edited by Edward Fenton
Illustrated by Malcolm Sparkes

DAY BOOKS
OXFORDSHIRE

ISBN 0 9532213 2 6

A catalogue record for this book is available from the British Library

Diary, autobiographical writings and photographs © Hana Pravda, 2000

Drawings © Malcolm Sparkes, 2000

This edition © Day Books, 2000

All rights reserved. This book is sold subject to the condition that it shall not, in whole or in part, be reproduced, copied or transmitted in any way without the publisher's prior consent in writing

Printed in England by the Information Press, Oxfordshire

Day Books, 3 Park Street, Charlbury, Oxfordshire OX7 3PS, UK.
www.day-books.com

Contents

Introduction

In the final months of World War II, the systematic extermination of Jews in the Nazi concentration camps was compounded by an additional horror: the phenomenon of the death march. From Auschwitz–Birkenau, Gleiwitz and dozens of smaller camps in the occupied territories, hundreds of thousands of prisoners were forced to march westwards, away from the Soviet advance. And even as some members of the SS tried desperately to destroy the evidence of their crimes—blowing up the gas chambers and crematoria—elsewhere their colleagues were continuing the massacres, on the roadsides and in the open railway-wagons bound for other concentration camps in the heart of Germany. According to even conservative estimates, at least 100,000 Jews died in this way: of hunger, or exposure, or murdered by the SS in cold blood.

Among those caught up in this misery was a young Czech actress who had been separated from her husband at Auschwitz, and who was now determined to find him again. Small and delicate-looking, she was nevertheless extremely robust, both mentally and physically. She herself ascribed her courage and resilience to her childhood diet of adventure stories and Karl May westerns: and indeed the story of her remarkable journey through

Josef and Beatrix Beck in 1915, shortly after their marriage.

the war zones of central Europe, from captivity to freedom, is itself worthy of one of the adventure books which so moulded her character.

Hana Beck was born at her grandparents' house in the Letná district of Prague, into a middle-class but by no means conventional Jewish family. She was an only child. Her father Dr Josef Beck had trained as a lawyer, but became a Cavalry officer in the Austro-Hungarian Army after the outbreak of the Great War, and was subsequently captured by the Russians. On his release he joined the newly formed Czechoslovak Legion and became embroiled in the Russian Civil War—finally returning home, via Vladivostok and Shanghai, in 1921. Years later, his daughter could remember vividly what she was doing when she saw him for the first time.

I was sitting on the carpet in our flat in Schneller Street, cutting up sheets of thick coloured paper—making paper dolls, and little dresses for them too. These creations of mine could even stand up if I bent the paper a bit at the bottom. Suddenly the door opened, and in came a stranger wearing a most peculiar outfit: a long grey coat, a grey fur cap, and a short sword at his side. My mother had tears in her eyes, but she looked overjoyed. 'This is your father, Hana!' she told me. 'Yes, your father!'

I didn't understand. I just stared at the stranger: and then he handed me a present, a heavy book full of pictures. After leafing through it, I started cutting out the pictures which most took my fancy. At first he didn't notice—but then suddenly he started yelling at me that I was spoiling a book of the finest reproductions from some famous art gallery. And I began to be afraid of him: and that fear has remained with me all my life.

'This is my family. Back row (from left to right): my grandfather Josef Stein, Aunt Olga, my mother, Aunt Roza, and my grandmother Anna Stein. Front row: Uncle Ota, myself with my dog Mitsi, and Uncle Franci (my mother's younger brother). I left out: Uncle Platovský, my two lovely cousins Jirka and Milan, and my father and his mother, because not everybody could fit in! Uncle Franci's wife and two children were left out as well.'

Hana's mother Beatrix, by contrast, was playful, kind and good-humoured. As Hana wrote later:

> I regarded her as my best friend, but she was also a goddess to me. Whatever she said and whatever she did was *right*. She played the piano to perfection and had a beautiful mezzo-soprano voice, and the only thing which stopped her from becoming a professional opera-singer was that it wouldn't have been proper for a girl from a respectable Jewish family to do so.
>
> My father would certainly have discouraged such a thing: just as, later, he discouraged my own ambitions to become an actress. 'I don't believe you belong on the stage at all,' he told me once. 'You are far too small!'

Hana's mother was still in her thirties when she started losing weight rapidly and becoming chronically tired. She was eventually diagnosed as having leukaemia, for which there was then no treatment; and her death, on 18th June 1932, created a new barrier between father and daughter.

> I felt my whole world irrevocably falling into a deep well of darkness: but not even then did my father try to comfort me. It was as if we were separated by some invisible glass wall.
>
> He didn't put his hands round my shoulders. He didn't press my hand. We were like two strangers, each of us alone in our pain.

Hana reacted by playing truant from school—taking the number 11 tram across Prague to the Jewish Cemetery in the Olšany district, where she would sit at her mother's graveside reading *War and Peace*. This continued for almost an entire term before her father found out. He then flew into a rage, and made Hana promise to go back and study until she had passed all her exams.

Hana Beck, aged sixteen.

As it turned out, it was fortunate that Hana returned to school: because it was through one of her schoolfriends, whose father was a scriptwriter, that she landed her first film role the following year. Karel Nový was looking for a young girl to play the juvenile lead in his film *Marijka Nevěrnice* (*Marijka the Unfaithful*): and his daughter told him that she had a classmate who was obsessed with acting. Since the filming was scheduled to take place during the summer holidays, Hana's father reluctantly allowed her to take part.

On its release in March 1934 the film was an immediate success, and this was all the encouragement Hana needed to make acting her career. She joined the municipal theatre company in

Hana Beck as the innkeeper's daughter in her first film, *Marijka Nevěrnice*, based on a story by Ivan Olbracht. It was filmed on location in the Carpathian Mountains, with members of the local peasantry appearing as extras and in some of the larger roles.

the Moravian city of Olomouc, and then in 1936 she travelled to the Soviet Union to attend drama school under the great director Alexei Dikii (1889–1955).

Hana was later to describe 1936 as 'that strange and thrilling year'—not just because of her Russian adventure, but also because this was the year when she fell suddenly in love.

One Sunday evening I went with two friends to a political meeting in Prague, organised by a group of law students who called themselves the Parliament of Youth. The hall was named after the composer Smetana, and it looked like a large theatre, with a balcony and gilded boxes. As I sat on the balcony, I found myself listening to

Sasha Munk, photographed by Hana Beck in the Tatry Mountains in the late summer of 1937. It was their first holiday together, and although they were not to get married for another two years, they called it their 'unofficial honeymoon'. Sasha Munk always hated having his picture taken, and only reluctantly agreed to pose for this shot.

an impassioned speech by a young man I had never seen before.

'Who *is* that man?' I asked my friend Ota Richter, who was sitting next to me.

'That's Sasha Munk,' he replied. 'But Hana—what's the matter with you? You look as if you've been struck by a brick. Are you all right?'

'I'm fine,' I assured him. 'But Ota, I have to talk to him!'

Ota looked puzzled, but he didn't ask any more questions. How could I possibly explain why I had to meet that fiery young man? I didn't understand it myself. All I knew was that I had instantly fallen deeply in love, and that I was certain I would soon marry that dark-eyed boy who had spoken so eloquently about justice in the world.

Equally surprising, as far as Hana Beck was concerned, was that Sasha Munk subsequently fell in love with her too. In 1939—soon after Hitler's invasion of Czechoslovakia—they got married, and moved to the beautiful village of Potštejn, deep in the Czech countryside. There, they believed, they would be safe; no one would know about Sasha Munk's previous association with the Parliament of Youth. As for Hana's acting career, it already seemed to be over: because, as a Jew, no theatre was now prepared to employ her.

Initially in Potštejn many of the anti-Jewish regulations were not rigorously enforced. As Hana wrote later: 'Apart from the order to wear those loathsome yellow stars on our clothes, they left us more or less in peace. Of course we had to give up our wireless set, our gramophone and our motor-car, but we could put up with all that.' Even when she was arrested briefly, in the summer of 1941, the incident struck her as more absurd than terrifying.

'You can imagine how embarrassing this is for me, madam,' the police officer kept saying. 'But I've got a written order from Gestapo headquarters in Kostelec. It says I have to take the Jewess Hana Munk into custody because she did something which it's strictly forbidden for Jews to do—she watched a football match.'

I burst out laughing. 'You mean the game between the boys in our village and the lads from Sopotnice? That wasn't a real match, it was only a bit of fun. Their ball kept going into the village pond because they were playing on such a steep slope! And you're really going to arrest me for that?'

'Of course,' said the policeman. 'The Gestapo is the Gestapo. Now I'm afraid I'll have to ask you to hurry up.'

All I could do was to scribble a note for my husband—'Don't worry, darling, they're just going to put me in prison for a few days for watching a football match'—and off we went.

The prison governor seemed embarrassed when we arrived. After escorting me to my cell, he assured me: 'Naturally I wouldn't dream of locking you in. The door will stay open and you can go wherever you want.'

But I didn't like the sound of that at all. 'I would much rather you locked me in, sir, just to be on the safe side. There may be some strange people around here.'

'Ah. You are quite right, madam. We have some quite nasty characters in here. I will certainly lock you in, if you wish.' Then he apologised to me, just as the policeman had done. 'All this is very painful for me, but I do hope you understand. After all, an order is an order. . . . '

Right: Sasha Munk in his reservist's uniform. In mid-1938 he and perhaps one and a half million other troops (sources differ as to the exact number) were sent to protect the Czech border from the threat of a German invasion, forming what Winston Churchill was later to describe as 'the strongest fortress line in Europe'. Following the Munich Conference at the end of September 1938, however, the Czech Army was demobilised and compelled to disarm.

The following May the assassination of Reinhard ('the hangman') Heydrich, the deputy head of Hitler's Gestapo, marked a turning-point in the Nazis' treatment of Jews in central Europe. The elimination of the Jewish people, which Heydrich had been at the forefront of planning, was now speeded up. Whole Jewish communities which had previously been untouched by the deportations were rounded up and sent to the death camps in the east. However, the operation was so huge that it took many months to complete: and, at first, life in Potštejn seemed largely unaffected. Although the Munks' home was searched following the assassination, once again the incident had an unreal quality about it.

The newly married Hana Munk in Potštejn—'an oasis of calm in the madhouse of Europe,' as she was later to describe it.

Of course the soldier couldn't find anything remotely suspicious in our little house, although he looked everywhere. At last he pulled a chair up to our dresser, handed me his loaded gun with its bayonet fixed, and barked an order: 'Halten Sie das für mich! Hold this for me!'

He climbed on to the chair and took down some heavy art books which I had bought years before at the Hermitage Museum in Leningrad. Then he sat down at our table and started leafing through them. 'Schön!' he murmured, as he looked at the pictures. 'Wunderschön!' And meanwhile I was standing next to him, holding his gun and thinking: 'Don't you realise I could just shoot you here, without any trouble?' And suddenly I felt sorry not just for myself, but for the young soldier as well.

It was not until the end of 1942 that 'Operation Reinhard'— as the package of reprisal measures was called—finally caught up with Hana and Sasha Munk. Shortly before Christmas, they and the other Jews in the district were rounded up and sent first to a transit camp in Prague.

There we were crammed into a large hall with about a thousand other prisoners, to await the orders of the SS men. Next to me, a grey-haired old lady was sitting on a bundle of clothes and clutching a large antique ear-trumpet. Suddenly one of the SS men marched up to her, yelling at her to 'Stand!'

Very calmly—very politely—the old lady put the ivory ear-trumpet to her ear, and said in perfect German, 'I'm sorry, what did you say? You must forgive me, I'm afraid I'm a little hard of hearing.'

The SS man kept barking out his order at the top of his voice, but to no effect. The old lady simply kept repeating that her hearing 'wasn't as good as it used to be', till finally he gave up and went to shout at someone else. And as the old lady settled down again on her bundle of clothes, I could hardly suppress a laugh, in spite of everything.

Poster for Karel Švenk's review, *Ať Žije Život*. The subtitle translates as 'Dancing around a skeleton'.

From Prague, the Munks were taken by train to the eighteenth-century garrison town of Terezín, which had been turned into a ghetto on the orders of Reinhard Heydrich himself. At the end of 1941 its small Czech population had been evacuated in preparation for the first trainloads of Jews, who were to be held captive there with minimal food and medication. In one month alone, September 1942, 4000 prisoners died of starvation. To relieve the pressure, 44,000 more were deported from Terezín to death camps in the east. Only three of them are known to have survived.

Yet despite the appalling conditions in Terezín, the creative spirit of its inhabitants could not be stifled. Concerts were staged; periodicals were published; artists continued to paint and draw; and when Hana Munk arrived, she became one of the moving forces behind the 'Freigeist' theatre group, which put on plays such as Goethe's *Faust* and Gogol's *Marriage*. Scripts were either smuggled in, or written from scratch. One of the most memorable was a musical entitled *Ať Žije Život* (*Long Live Life*), written by a young internee called Karel Švenk, who did not survive the War.

'Art is not a luxury,' Hana was to say later. 'It is a necessity.' It was a way of enabling herself and the people around her to imagine a world beyond the everyday realities of starvation, disease and death.

Unfortunately, any sense of stability created in this way was largely illusory. Of the 140,000 people who were transported to Terezín between 1941 and 1945, about a quarter died there, while well over half were later deported to concentration camps in occupied Poland and elsewhere.

After almost two years in Terezín, it was finally Sasha Munk's turn to be deported east, to Auschwitz: and Hana, unable to contemplate being separated from him, volunteered to go too. Neither of them had any idea what lay in store for them; for as soon as they arrived at Auschwitz, on 1st October 1944, the men and women were divided up and sent off in different directions.

I and the other girls were herded into a cold cement hall, where a battalion of hefty female Stormtroopers started shaving our heads in a kind of fury. It was extremely painful—but then suddenly the woman who was shaving me stopped, and I saw that she was looking down at my leather boots.

'If you give me your boots,' she whispered to me, 'if you give them now, before they get mixed up with everyone else's shoes, I won't shave the rest of your head.'

'But then I'll have long hair on one side and be bald on the other!' I told her. 'No thanks. Shave it all off, please.'

So she did.

Because she was still relatively strong, despite her years of internment, Hana Munk was not sent to the gas chambers. Instead, after just a few days in Auschwitz, she was put on another train with several hundred other women and girls, and sent over 200 miles north-west to a small town called Trachenburg (in Polish, Żmigród).

As they got off the train, some of the girls were terrified that they were about to be shot: but Hana Munk pointed out that they would hardly have been transported so far when they could have been murdered more easily at Auschwitz. And indeed, from Trachenburg they were marched to the nearby military camp of Birnbäumel, where they were set to work, building defences and digging trenches to try and stop the Russian tanks. Hana was unaware that she was just part of a far larger chain of about 10,000 women and girls, at a dozen similar camps nearby, who were being forced to construct a huge fault-line across the landscape. It was only after three months of exhausting labour

Hana Munk used the back of her diary to jot down addresses, lists, and (as in this photograph) snatches of poetry.

that it became clear to their captors that these measures were futile, and the camp was abandoned: and this is the point at which Hana Munk's diary begins.

The core of the diary was written over the next five months, during which it became a tool for her very survival. As the fighting raged all around her, she used it to counteract the chaos and the brutalisation—filling its pages with her reflections on art and literature, with descriptions of everyday comforts which she had been deprived of for so long, and above all with her hopes for the future. And it is this emphasis on hope which, despite the tragedy, makes the diary ultimately such an inspiring and life-affirming document.

EDWARD FENTON

GERMANY

Wohlau
(Wolów)

Dyhernfur
(Brzeg Do

Dresden●

●Terezín

●Kraslice

Prague
●

●Cheb

BOHEMIA

Kutná Hora
●

Potšte
●

MORAVI/

Brno●

●Munich

AUSTRIA

Vienna
●

0		100 km
0	50 km	

Central Europe at the time of Hana Munk's journey from captivity. (Dotted line

Birnbäumel
(Gruszeczka)
●

POLAND

reslau   ● Kępno
Vrocław)

River Odra

● Częstochowa

Kielce
●

Sandomierz ●

Rozwadów
●

Gleiwitz
(Gliwice)
●   ● Kattowitz
(Katowice)

River Wisła

● Auschwitz
(Oświecim)

Chyrów
●

● Olomouc

B E S K I D Y   M O U N T A I N S

Prešov
●

S L O V A K I A

Košice
●

● Uzhhorod

Třebišov

ratislava

HUNGARY

ndicate Czechoslovak borders before partition, September–November 1938.)

All things in life occur by chance:
One day you're up, then down you'll be;
Life flows like water's liquid dance,
Till at the end you reach the sea.

We all must drift into that sea,
Some sooner, others later on.
Let all those touched by love be free,
And know that hope is never gone.

For life's like water, fresh and pure,
Which love alone turns into wine.
Though love itself is never sure,
It touches us with joy divine.

From 'Život je jen náhoda'
by Jiří Voskovec and Jan Werich;
translated by Riitta Heino and Alex Pravda.

DIARY
1945

21st–26th January

I'm now going to write down some of the things which have happened over the last few days. I've got such a short memory, I'm afraid, and this is a way of making sure that I don't forget.

It was on Sunday that the order came to leave the camp where we'd been held—the women's labour camp at Birnbäumel, a kilometre from Sulau in south-western Poland. There were nine hundred of us when we set off.

The Russian Army has been getting closer all the time, so the Germans are on the run: and they're taking us with them. We're being guarded by about fifteen German Schupos—SS and SA men. There are three women Schupos too. Their commander is Oberscharführer Josef something-or-other. . . . I don't know his full name.

The first big place we passed was Breslau. It was in the middle of being evacuated, so we had to skirt round it. We met a French prisoner of war who told us that the Russians were only 20 kilometres away.

After that we had to march for miles through a completely deserted and barren expanse of land. Many of the girls from our transport have been trying to hide in the abandoned houses. Three of them were found and executed on the spot.

We crossed the River Odra on a pontoon bridge near Dyhernfurth—all the other bridges have been blown up. The bridge had been covered in land-mines to try and stop the Russian advance.
Then at last we
found

ourselves in a populated part of the country once again.

We are starving. The only food we have had on the whole march has been a few drops of milk, two raw beetroots and five raw potatoes.

27th January

Today we were given a taste of soup for the first time since leaving Birnbäumel. We've been locked up in an old factory where some sort of iron tools used to be made. All the workers have fled.

We all feel completely exhausted. This is the first warm place we've been in since we set off, and it's making us feel quite drunk. All around me the other girls are taking off the dirty rags we've been wearing, and I'm horrified to see that they look like skeletons.

The girls who couldn't carry on marching have already been shot. That's what happened to the purest and best soul in the world, Anči Vinklerová from Prague. The horrors of the march must have driven her mad, because yesterday she just sat down on the road and refused to carry on. Four of us tried desperately to pick her up, but it was impossible. She kept slipping through our hands, back onto the frozen road. Her eyes were glazed—expressionless—as if she were staring into another world. . . . And still she wouldn't move.

Meanwhile the Schupos kept shouting at us to hurry up, and at last we had to leave her lying in the snow. Two or three minutes later we heard a shot, and that was the end of Anči.

I think they've shot about fifteen girls, but a lot more are missing. Altogether we've lost about 350 people.

We're as hungry as wolves. When they marched us out to the soup-vats, we began fighting in the snow for a few frozen cabbage-leaves.

Whatever happens, I've got to escape. I have nothing to lose. It's clear that we're already done for.

I start looking around for hiding-places,

but it seems hopeless. There are some old water-pipes covered in snow . . . but the SS men are watching us far too closely.

Of all the girls here, I feel I can trust Vera Kornová the most. We've been talking about trying to escape—but so far, we haven't had a chance.

28th January

Vera tells me that today would have been her mother's birthday. She comes across one of the girls wearing her mother's old jacket, and in one of the pockets she finds a hand-written ticket from one of the theatre-shows we used to stage in the Terezín ghetto. It has the word 'Freigeist' on it, which is what we used to call our drama group—'Free spirit.'

'Your mother's trying to send you a greeting,' I tell Vera. 'It's a good omen!'

But Vera just goes on crying.

We've been kept locked up in the factory all day. We had to sleep on a thick layer of iron-dust under a wrought-iron table—and it's there, in the dust, that we plan our escape.

29th January

My birthday.

During the night some water-pipes burst in the lavatory. In the darkness the running water sounded like a raging ocean, and we started shouting and screaming to try and wake the guards: but it was useless. We were trapped in our concrete prison.

Thank God, when dawn came, we found that the water had been running much more slowly than we'd imagined. Only half of the room was flooded.

Anyway, now it's time to pull on our rags again. The Schupos are yelling at us to hurry up.

Lying under the table, I start singing: 'Život je jen náhoda—All things in life occur by chance.' Stela Gráfová is lying next to me, and she gives me a birthday present—half a carrot, which was her last bit of food. That's more than Vera and I had between us!

Someone comes and tells us that we're leaving the factory this morning.

We go outside. The Germans are going to hand round some potatoes.

Suddenly I realise that nobody is watching us. I tell Vera, 'This is our chance' and then I find myself running—in fact not running but walking, very calmly, round the corner to the back of the factory. And Vera is following me!

Then all we can do is wait. We wait in the deep snow for what seems like an eternity. We are freezing. Will the column never move off?

We run over to the railway tracks to hide behind a big pile of bricks. By now we are completely frozen through. Vera can't stand the tension, and keeps peeping out from our hiding-place.

At last they finish distributing the potatoes, and the prisoners begin to move slowly away.

In the middle distance, behind a frozen stream, we can see a large villa. It appears to be deserted. We decide to try and reach it, and then we start fantasising about what it'll be like inside. Perhaps we'll find some potatoes there! Perhaps we'll be able to wash!

So we set off towards it, but the snow is so deep that it's almost impossible to walk, and we keep tripping over things hidden underfoot. We're exhausted.

Then we find our path blocked by a barbed-wire fence: and beyond the fence, the snow is even deeper. We weren't prepared for anything like that. We are going to try the road to the village instead.

Suddenly we catch sight of one of our SA Schupos riding a bicycle towards us. He yells at us: 'Was macht ihr denn da? Wo habt ihr die Nummern?' Then he says: 'Dort im Walde werdet ihr erschossen! Und die Krähen werden eure Augen fressen!'*

And then he starts chasing us. Three or four boys— members of the local Hitler Youth—start chasing us too, and manage to surround us. They must be about fourteen or sixteen years old.

I beg the Schupo to shoot me on the spot. The icy wind is cutting right through me, and I've had enough.

The Schupo slaps my face and I fall flat on my back, not so much from the blow as from exhaustion. I fall straight under his bicycle. He grabs me by the collar and lifts me up,

*'What are you doing here? Where are your numbers? . . . I'll shoot you there in the forest and the crows will peck your eyes out!'

and we walk on. Vera hisses at me: 'Don't be so melodramatic!'

Three of the Hitler Youth boys are still following us. They ask the Schupo if they can help him. He tells them, 'Die werden sowieso erschossen—they will be shot anyway.'

At last the boys drift away, and the Schupo starts walking faster. I realise suddenly that I know him from the camp. By a strange coincidence his name is the same as my husband's—Sasha.

Sasha. . . . No German would have a name like that. So I start thinking: perhaps he has a Polish mother. And then I remember something else—his mother is dead. In fact, that's why I recognise him. About a week before we were marched out of Birnbäumel, he was running about from tent to tent, shouting that his entire family had been killed in the bombing of Breslau. He looked desperate.

Now I watch him as he goes on pushing his bicycle uphill along the icy road: and as his pace quickens it's almost as if *he* wants to escape from *us*. We stumble along behind him, and Vera keeps falling down. I feel miserable for her.

The road is covered in ice. All around us there is nothing but a white desert swept by an icy wind. It's a wasteland. And then Sasha starts running. He's going faster and faster. An old peasant comes by, driving a hay-cart, and I beg him to let us on: but the old man just responds with a curse.

At the top of the hill we see the first cottages of a village. Sasha isn't looking back. It's obvious that he's giving us the chance to escape. I whisper to Vera, 'If he turns left, then we'll turn right.'

I feel completely calm—strangely calm—and deep inside me I can feel, once again, a tiny spark of hope.

We approach the village slowly. The road leads straight ahead, without a turning—but suddenly Sasha is nowhere to be seen. He has vanished.

A little girl is standing in front of the first cottage on the right. I ask her, 'Ist die Mutti zu Hause? Is your mummy at home?' and I hear a calm, sweet 'Ja.'

We go inside—and immediately I have an urge to rush upstairs and hide. But then a small round-faced woman, about forty years old, emerges from one of the ground-floor rooms and asks what we're looking for.

For the first time my nerve fails me. Vera and I both start jabbering hysterically about people wanting to shoot us, and how she's got to let us in.

She closes the front door and leads us into the kitchen, and we tell her everything. Then she shows us into her living-room, where there is a child's bed, a fire burning in the tiled stove, and a big old-fashioned wall-clock ticking peacefully away.

She goes out, and returns with mugs of hot milk and slices of bread and Sana margarine. As I cradle the bread in the palm of my hand, I start sobbing with happiness and gratitude. I can see by the big wooden clock that it's just half past ten in the morning, and already I've met my

second real human being of the day—first the Schupo
Sasha, and now this woman.

But I know it's dangerous for her to keep us in the
cottage, and she knows it too. She tells us that the local
teacher, who is a real Nazi, lives in the house on the left. We
are lucky not to have turned left.

'So what can we do?' we ask.

She points across the road to a large building that used to
be the village poor-house. She explains that the house is now
full of Polish and Russian slave-labourers from the occupied

territories who are all working for local farmers. We promise to go there when it starts to get dark.

Just before lunchtime the little girl returns. Her mother makes lunch—four eggs for the little girl, and some goat's meat and beans for us. It tastes wonderful, but I'm too embarrassed to be seen scraping out the pot. Although I'm starving, I can't bring myself to do it.

After the meal we offer to wash up—and what pleasure that gives us! It feels like celebrating mass, or offering up a prayer of thanks for the return of life.

Frau Milde—that's her name—offers us some pancakes, but we say no. We know she has little enough herself. Then in the afternoon she goes out: and when she is gone, I run into the little entrance-hall and tear my thin coat into tiny pieces. I hate doing it, but it's better to freeze than be given away by the red lacquered crosses they painted on us all before the march.

Through the cottage windows I can see wagons rolling by, some large, some small, but all full of retreating Germans. Then Frau Milde comes back weeping, and we find ourselves—wretched as we are—trying to cheer her up! She tells us that her husband is a soldier on the Russian front, and she doesn't know if he's alive or dead.

She offers us some hot milky coffee, and Sana margarine on bread.

Outside, as it grows dark, we see that it's snowing. It's half past five. We feel it's time to say goodbye and go.

Frau Milde presses a German coin into my hand, and into Vera's too—one German mark each. I kiss her hand and we go out, as if in a dream, into the windswept night.

At the door of the big house opposite I find a sturdy big-boned woman, and I speak to her in Russian. She lets us in.

The building is packed. Two Ukrainian men come in carrying half a dead calf. 'Don't ask where we got it from!' they say. They start playing a game of cards, and I offer to read the cards for them all. I tell the woman that she will see the man she loves very soon.

'That's impossible,' she replies.

30th January

Out of the blue, the sturdy woman's husband arrives on a big grey horse. I have now become a 'white witch', and everyone wants to know their fortune. They bring me a piece of pork for my magic!

These people know what it is to be hungry. We are so thin, but they don't ask why. Instead they ply us with milk and calf's-foot jelly, and can't understand why it gives us such terrible diarrhoea.

3rd February

We stayed in the house opposite Frau Milde's cottage for five days without being disturbed: but then today a Nazi official arrived without warning. It was the same Nazi teacher who Frau Milde had told us about. He was also the Bürgermeister's secretary. He was wearing a uniform and holding a pistol.

When he asked us for our papers, Vera replied in her excellent German, and calmly trotted out the story we had prepared. We were both teachers from Czechoslovakia, she told him, and we'd been sent here as forced-labourers, like thousands of others.

He ordered us not to move from this house. 'Ich werde Ordnung schaffen,' he said. 'I'll put this in order!'

4th February

Today the Bürgermeister's secretary appeared again with some other official. They both swallowed our fairy-tale, and said that we could go to work at the big farm. They even offered us a little place to stay up there.

As a special favour the secretary gave us an official document which allowed us to get a loaf of bread each, and later he came back with two printed food-coupons, the 'Essenkarten'.

8th February

We worked on the big farm for five days. We had to milk the cows and muck out the cow-sheds.

I was no good at milking—I was so frightened of hurting the poor creatures. It was the same with mucking out. When one of the cows refused to move, I tried talking to her, and prodded her gently with the handle of a pitchfork, but she took no notice. An old German farm-worker laughed at me, and dug the prongs into the cow's body until at last she moved slowly away. 'That's how to do it,' he said. 'No use talking to her!'

Suddenly a young Ukrainian boy called Nikita burst into the cow-shed. 'Come and have a look!' he was shouting. 'There are soldiers outside!'

It would have been dangerous for us to leave the farm, but I rushed over to the fence. I could hear the noise of approaching tanks. Nikita thought they must be Germans, but suddenly I saw three Russian soldiers outside.

I couldn't believe my eyes. I ran over to them, weeping with joy, then led them inside so that Vera could see them too. We offered them food but they didn't want anything; all they wanted was some hot coffee.

It was then that I realised all the Germans had disappeared. Only the old farm-worker with the pitchfork had stayed behind. He explained that he wasn't scared of the Russians.

'What have I got to lose?' he said. 'On this estate here they never paid me. All they gave me was my food, and a pair of high boots once a year. I'm staying put. No one can steal what I haven't got.'

9th–12th February

Vera and I stayed two more days in the deserted village. We took whatever we could from the houses of the Nazi teacher and the inspector. Even Frau Milde had fled. Apart from us, only the Poles and the Russians had stayed behind. And now we all wanted to move on too, away from the front, away from the noise of the guns, away from the drunken soldiers.

In the end we set off with a wagon to try and make our way to liberated Poland.

At first we had no idea which way to go: but when we reached a crossroads, we received some help from an unexpected source. There, leaning against a telegraph pole, was a very fat and very frozen dead pig. One of its legs was propping up a piece of cardboard, with the words: 'THIS WAY TO BERLIN.' So immediately we set off in the opposite direction.

We crossed the River Odra again, and at night we slept on the open wagon. Sometimes we got rained on, and one dark night—lit up only by the light of the rockets and the bombs—it started to snow very heavily. I was furious. I shook my fist at the sky and yelled: 'Stop it! Stop it at once'—and the snow stopped! That scared me a bit.

We only had one horse, and when our cart got stuck in the deep mud and sludge along the River Odra, we had to abandon most of the things we'd looted. Then a young Russian soldier suddenly appeared as if from nowhere and ordered us to give him our strong black horse. In return he left us with his stubborn long-haired pony, which absolutely refused to be harnessed to our wagon. Try as we might, we could do nothing with that beastly kicking pony. In the end we had to let him go.

So there we were, without a horse and with our cart stuck deep in the river mud. We rescued two small bundles from it, and one of the Polish families on our wagon-train—Mr Dadek and Marie Kudwadž from Kraków—agreed to carry them for us. We had to follow their wagon on foot. They were already carrying two small children and an aunt and a grandmother. The grandmother was a godsend, because she wore a bright red scarf on her head, so we could always see their cart even if we got held up or started lagging behind.

Altogether there must have been twenty wagons at least.

We passed through one village after another, and at night we slept in the deserted houses. Mr Dadek was only interested in finding proper stables for his two horses. Where the rest of us slept didn't bother him at all.

One evening, in our mad innocence, Vera and I nearly fell into the lion's den. . . . We were like two frail eggshells, and only God saved us from harm.

What happened was that we accepted an invitation from a group of Russian officers to share a meal with them. They sang to us quite beautifully, but then they started being a real nuisance, and goodness knows what would have happened if I hadn't been able to speak to them forcefully in their own language. I begged them to leave Vera alone, to think of their mothers and sisters and respect her as a virgin. They did stop pestering her—but then one of them, guessing correctly that I *wasn't* a virgin, started to chase me.

We were in a big barn two storeys high, and I ran up to the second floor and he followed me. There was a lot of grain upstairs, and in the middle of the floor was a big hole above the threshing-floor. And as he chased me, I made up my mind to push him through the hole, in the hope of killing him. So perhaps we're all capable of committing murder. . . . Anyway, the soldier must have realised, because he gave up the chase.

13th February

My husband's birthday.

We are at a railway-station, somewhere called Wohlau. There are heaps of bags and cases piled around everywhere.

Because we didn't have any papers, we were trying to stay in the background—and then suddenly in the middle of the road I saw a huge leg of smoked pork! I cut off as much meat as I could. It was delicious.

In the evening we found another Czech refugee in one of the little houses. His name was Mr Michálek, and he came from Unhošt. He told us that the Russians had taken all his papers.

We trudged on through the deep mud. There were dead bodies all around us: dead Germans and Russians, and countless dead animals too—horses, cows, pigs, geese, dogs—corpses by the hundred, and wrecked vehicles everywhere. I even saw a beautiful white American-made ambulance being kicked by an angry Russian soldier, who was cursing it just as he might curse his horse. Finally he left it in the snow, with all its supply of medicines and instruments just lying there.

I pocketed a pair of shiny scissors, and felt as if I was stealing a diamond—except that it was even more precious, because it was so much more useful.

14th February–7th March

We've just spent the night in a beautiful large villa with a piano. I've already requisitioned a picture of Beethoven that I found there. In another villa I changed into clean underwear—but all the dresses that had been left behind were enormous.

On the dressing-table there was a box of face-powder, which smelt exactly like the powder that my wonderful drama teacher Olga Scheinpflugová used to wear. But when I looked at my face in the mirror, it was the face of a stranger. My hair is only just growing back, and now I've got thick black eyebrows which I never had before.

I decided that I couldn't put any powder on such a face, so I emptied the box into my boots, just to carry its perfume with me. But I did take some clean underwear, and a real down duvet for Vera. There's only straw in the house where she's sleeping now.

In all the big deserted houses we've been finding discarded SA and SS uniforms lying on the floor, like snakeskins that have been sloughed off. There's always plenty of food, too. It makes the mouth water: bags of rice,

fruit preserves neatly labelled from 1938 right up to 1944, lots of coffee and tins of cocoa. There are hardly any books, but plenty of musical instruments—pianos and guitars.

In one house I found two books: *Gösta Berling* by Selma Lagerlöf, and *Don Quixote*. Otherwise the main reading-matter seems to consist of magazines for Army officers and members of the Nazi party.

Outside, desperate animals are roaming the length and breadth of the vast snow-covered plains. The cows are lowing miserably because they are absolutely dying to be milked. The Poles are catching them and tying them to their carts.

And strange little incidents keep on happening. On the second day of our stay beside the river, I noticed a Russian soldier on duty at the crossroads, playing the accordion and dancing. He danced beautifully. There were dead bodies all around; not far away the big guns were booming, and the village next to the river was on fire. They call the guns 'Stalin's organ'.

After a great deal of pleading, Vera was allowed to sit on one of the wagons for a while because of the festering wound on her leg: but I had to walk behind the cart all the way. I found myself making up all sorts of jokes and songs to try and forget about my lacerated left foot.

At one point I gave the driver a jar of cocoa-powder that I'd found. Before I could say anything, he put a great spoonful into his mouth—and started to choke!

As soon as he'd recovered he threw the jar away, shouting at me and accusing me of trying to kill him. The poor man had obviously never seen cocoa in his life. Then he asked me contemptuously how I could eat 'that tinned rubbish' that I'd brought from the villas. Why didn't I kill one of the chickens running around on the road, and have some *proper* food?

I had to confess that I couldn't bring myself to kill them.

He laughed, took a stick and threw it like a boomerang, hitting a chicken about ten metres away and killing it instantly.

Anyway, when we stopped at one of the deserted villages that evening, we all had the most delicious chicken soup. 'You can't kill the damn things,' the Polish man barked at me, 'but you don't have any trouble eating them!' So he was a kind man really, giving us all that delicious chicken soup.

On the same dirty road I came across a doll. Its blonde hair had started to become unglued, so I pulled it off and put it under my headscarf, which I'd made from the artificial silk lining of my coat. The doll's blonde wig hung down over my forehead, hiding my shaved prisoner's head. The next day one of the Polish women pleaded with me to sell her my scarf. She said she liked the colour—red. I just ran away from her.

I can still hear her voice: 'Ma pani coś do sprzedania—have you got anything to sell, lady?'

At last we reached a village called Kępno, where we waited for a train all afternoon and all the following day. When it eventually arrived, it turned out to be a goods train.

Vera and I sneaked on to one of the open carriages and tried to find a little space among all the pots and pans on board. They were incredibly uncomfortable to sit on. And then the Poles we've been travelling with got angry with us, because they were so concerned about the welfare of their precious pots.

One afternoon we saw a group of male prisoners walking past in the distance—too far away to talk to. They were clutching their grey prison blankets round their bodies, and all we could see of their faces were their huge staring eyes. They moved as slowly as ghosts. Would I recognise my Sasha among them? Would he recognise me?

I think about him all the time.

At noon the next day we reached the River Stradomca, on the edge of Częstochowa. There I exchanged a brown skirt for half a loaf of white bread and ten cigarettes. Then I gave Vera's bundle to Mr Michálek to look after, and we limped on into town with the Polish refugees.

At Częstochowa we were directed to a street called Kilinskiego, where Vera and I somehow got separated. When we found each other again, we'd both been crying. We reached the Czech hostel as tired as kittens. The address was 62 Washington Strasse. I didn't expect anything special; all I wanted to do was sleep.

Suddenly I noticed two old friends from Terezín: Rudy Freudenfeld (the one we used to call Pařík—'Piglet'—) and Karel Kavan. I thought I must be dreaming and that I would awake at any minute. I just stared at them, and realised that I wasn't imagining it. They were really there.

Later I discovered some other people I knew as well—some girls from our sister camp of Kreuzbach.

8th March

My friends Gusta Schwarzkopf and Pat'a Fischl have arrived from Kattowitz. They told me that Honza Fischer was slightly wounded in Blechhammer, and that he has now gone with a few other people to Slovakia.

I'm still asking everyone about Sasha, but all I've heard is that he was chosen—as an exceptionally strong and athletic man—to join a special group working in a munitions factory. Apparently his transport was sent to a factory near Leipzig. . . . But as for when he left, or where he is now, I have no idea.

Dear God, look after him and bring him back to me. That's all I'm asking—I don't want anything else!

9th March

Today I went with Gusta Schwarzkopf to the famous Jasná Hill. I have visited the magnificent church three times already, but Gusta was so knowledgeable that today it

seemed transformed. Near the great old church organ on the balcony he gave me a fascinating lecture on the development of European art and the styles of different historical periods. A host of little white angels seemed to be smiling at us from above the left altar. Outside it was the most glorious winter's day, with the virgin snow shimmering in the sunlight.

In the evening I translated an indictment of a man called Bernstein into Russian. He was the worst, cruellest and most sadistic of the Schupos from the Gleiwitz 1 prison camp, and our boys just happened to find him in the local hospital. At last, the chance for a bit of revenge!

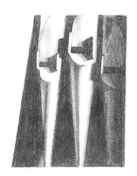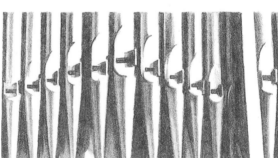

The Russians assure us that we'll be leaving soon. Vera and I have moved to a street known as Freedom Alley, no. 11.

The Czech hostel in Washington Strasse was a former school, and we slept on some overturned bookcases. Now in Freedom Alley we've got a bare little room which the Germans have abandoned. We are sharing it with some Polish Jews. They are being quite polite, but they can't hide the fact that they didn't actually invite us.

We can't wait to leave.

10th March

Today Pat'a dropped in and we had a nice long talk.

I tried to ask Pat'a about how he'd escaped, but he didn't want to talk about it. He said he couldn't—not now—and asked me to tell him about my experiences instead. I didn't mind talking about some of the more absurd situations. They were so painful, but that didn't stop them from being funny sometimes.

I must have a weird sense of humour. I can't help it.

I told him about how the Germans made us dig a trench to try and stop the Russian tanks. It was about three metres deep, with water at the bottom, and our SS men thought it highly amusing to push us into the water as we dug. They absolutely hooted with laughter when Mrs Müller went tumbling in. She still looked quite fat in her rags—in spite of being starved—and she was incredibly clumsy. Climbing out of the trench, soaking wet, in about 10 degrees below zero—well, that wasn't funny, but somehow she survived their sport.

Another way the SS men amused themselves was by setting their dogs on us while we slept in our tents.

We used to sleep under big paper bags. We were all crawling with lice, and I discovered that if I undressed completely and put my rags on top of me, the lice got half-frozen and stopped biting. Unfortunately, the moment I got dressed they woke up again and started tucking in to their breakfast—me. I think that having lice was worse than being hungry.

At last Pat'a did tell me a few things, although obviously not the worst of them. He described how the boys in his camp used to talk for hours about cooking. Our girls did the same, all day long. It drove me crazy.

While we were digging that stupid trench, I remember, I decided to give the five other girls in my group a crash-course on the history of art. I managed to get as far as the beginning of the seventeenth century before the Russians came too close. I talked so much that I almost lost my voice, but the girls seemed to enjoy it.

Apart from digging that useless trench we had to cut down trees, and the local Polish woodcutters used to watch our efforts with a mixture of pity and despair. They tried to show us how to do it properly, but it was no use. One of them gave me a big juicy onion, which I ate like an apple.

On other occasions, for some unknown reason, we were

made to unload truckloads of bricks. I can still feel the weight of the bricks that were thrust at me, four at a time, for me to pass on.

Some girls in our camp died of typhus. We made a little cemetery for them. In spite of being Jewish we marked the graves with crosses. Then the twelve-year-old daughter of our Kapo caught the disease, so in the daytime we used to hide her under a heap of our paper sleeping-bags. She was a very tall child, so the Nazis believed our lie that she was sixteen—otherwise they would have executed her, like everyone else who wasn't strong enough to work.

Our Kapo, Eva, was a beautiful young Hungarian Jewess with a kind temperament, and she was grateful to us all for trying to save her child, so we had no trouble from her.

In the forest surrounding the labour camp I found some sweet red cranberries: so pure and beautiful, like messages from another world. But it was impossible to run away. Where could I have gone?

Talking to Pat'a today cheered me up. He is a real friend. But now our departure has been delayed again. There is a rumour that the bridge over the River Wisła has fallen down.

13th March

This morning I went to Russian command section 106 to fill in some forms which have to be sent to Moscow. Afterwards I sold my lovely black embroidered Ukrainian jacket on the black market near the church. I'll always remember it with affection.

Then I went to a patisserie with my friend Roza, and spent 50 of the 100 zloty I got for it. A single piece of cake cost 15 zloty. For the first time in three years we were sitting at a table in a patisserie! There were no plates or spoons, of course, and we had to ask twice just to get a glass of water.

Today I met Dr Krause, a little stick of a man with glasses, whose bunk had been next to Sasha's in Terezín. Dear God, I am meeting everyone except the one person I really love!

In the afternoon I went to see a sort of variety show put on by a Russian theatre group. There was one good baritone. Then they put on a short play by Anton Chekhov. Chekhov is always irresistible.

I must also tell you that I've already seen three films since I've been here. The first one—an American film with Joel McCrea and Andrea Leeds—was so unbelievably stupid that we couldn't stop laughing. The women had so much make-up on that they all looked identical. They had no personality whatever. They looked like tailor's dummies in a shop window.

One of the other films was a Russian musical about the war. It was called *Lezginka*. It was so naive—trying to represent this horrific time in an absurdly idealised and sanitised way.

I have forgotten to mention how we celebrated our late President Masaryk's birthday on 7th March. We had a wonderful picture of Masaryk, which someone had drawn in chalk on green paper—and we sang songs and recited Baroque poems, including Erik Saudek's beautiful lines:

One day our suffering will cease,
One day the jug of tears will break,
One day will water turn to wine,
One day will death its prey forsake.

Mr Fiala made a good speech. It was the first free celebration we'd had in six whole years.

14th March

We are about to leave this place. The Russians have been promising this for days now, and finally we're going. So now I'd better go and sell a blouse to buy some bread. That's all I've got left to sell.

I wish I knew which way we're heading—and where we're going to end up. The Russians spent this morning loading some Serbian refugees on to the train.

15th March

When at last it was time to say goodbye, I went out into the courtyard. Farewell, Częstochowa.

It is exactly six years since Hitler invaded Czechoslovakia. I pray that this train will bring us home to Bohemia—one way or another.

16th March

The train rattles on and on. Our carriage is packed to bursting. We slept as well as could be expected.

It's a military train—no seats, just benches along the sides and a small stove in the middle of the floor. There are twenty-one of us altogether in this carriage.

Vera has changed. She's not the same girl that she was. For some reason she is withdrawing into herself. And then suddenly, God knows why, she'll explode at me. She took my blanket from me—and then it was *her* who was angry with *me*! What have I done to upset her? I suppose we're all feeling tired and irritable.

In the morning we stopped off to have a wash, but now we are travelling again. We are on the way to Kielce. There are sheep and shepherds everywhere—little houses and wooden cottages are dotted about—and there's still a lot of snow.

Now the sun is shining. Last night I dreamt about Sasha. May God look after him, wherever he is.

17th–19th March

The countryside around us is changing. No more snow, only grey and yellow grass. There are deep trenches everywhere. Every so often we see graves marked with wooden discs painted red—graves of Russian soldiers. There are wrecked cars and tanks and ambulances all about us, and for a while we run alongside a wartime communications system—a few wires strung between some bits of birch-wood.

I'm bored. Somebody has given me a book by Edgar Allan Poe. We're just coming up to the River Wisła.

The old bridge across the Wisła has been destroyed, so a pontoon bridge has been put there instead. The bridge is very low, and the river water is splashing over it.

About thirty lorries are waiting on the riverside, half-submerged in the bottomless Polish mud. Slowly we step out of the train. It's very dark, and everyone puts their bags in a pile to make a sort of landmark. We are horrified when we realise suddenly that we have been stacking our bags on a freshly dug grave.

In this war one finds graves in the most unlikely places. Here at the railway-station, for instance. I slip, and fall back into the thick mud.

As a special favour, Vera and I have been found places in the second lorry, with about twenty other people. I have a little boy called Pepíček on my lap. I'm clutching him tight because the driver is going so fast. Pepíček is a golden child, incredibly quiet.

I've got an agonising pain in my stomach. Our driver is a maniac. I start praying to myself: 'Good Lord—deliver us!'

After driving some distance—perhaps seven kilometres, perhaps seventeen, I don't know—we get out at another railway-station, and are loaded onto a waiting train, about fifty people to a carriage. We have to sleep on wooden pallets, about eight of us together.

The next morning we heard some terrible news. One of the lorry-drivers stopped his truck in front of the bridge, went to a tavern and drank a whole bottle of vodka. He was so drunk that when he got back into the lorry he went swerving off the bridge half-way across, and ended up with his front wheels in the water and the back wheels only just hanging on to the bridge.

In his madness he ignored the people who were trying to jump out of the lorry: he stepped on the accelerator and tried to drive on, tearing away a piece of the bridge, so that the people closest to the edge fell into the icy water and drowned. They say that eighteen people were killed, and only two of the passengers were saved because they were somewhere else at the time.

We don't know who the dead people were, but apparently they were from the Free Slovak Army. There was also one boy from Prague. They were all young people. How dreadful to die now—for nothing.

Yet I believe that everything's in God's hands, all the good and terrible things, just like in the book *The Bridge of San Luis Rey*—even if it doesn't make sense to us just now.

The station, incidentally, was called Sandomierz.

We are now missing 140 people and all our provisions. A lot of people were thrown out of the lorries and had to make their way here on foot. Many of them must still be walking.

Perhaps they'll get here soon.

We are heading towards the town of Lwów. Today we are near a village called

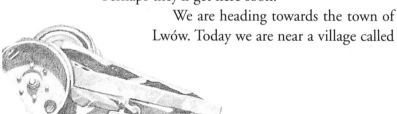

Rozwadów. We can hear music coming from somewhere.

Some of the girls are smoking and making toast. Vera and I are eating what's left of our last loaf of bread.

The little stove is warm and comforting. Yesterday we were given no food at all. I wonder what's going to happen next?

19th March, 3 p.m.

There are rumours that we'll be moving off again in a couple of hours. This is our second day at Rozwadów, and we like it here.

Yesterday, because we had no provisions, we were sent off into the forest to see what we could find. Half-way there we came across a large farm which has been turned into an officers' mess, so we ate there. We went back there again today.

We had a table for six, though there were no plates, knives or forks.

We were given bowls of soup with crackling and mushrooms, then some porridge made out of goodness knows what, then four lumps of sugar and four pieces of bread.

It was wonderful to sit at a table and be waited on. An officer drove us back—Vera, Pepíček, Professor Spicer and me. The thick mud everywhere no longer bothers us, and it feels fantastic to be driven in a car, even if it is only an Army jeep.

When we woke up this morning they sent us off to be bathed and disinfected in a special train opposite our own. The men had already had their turn yesterday evening and on into the night.

The hot water and clean clothes felt heavenly. Our dresses and coats came out very stiff from the detergent and steam, but we didn't care. All the lice were dead.

Apparently the reports about the catastrophe at the bridge were exaggerated. Only one person was drowned, and two are missing; the others who fell into the river were rescued by the Russian soldiers.

We've also heard that our brave Czech boys—eighteen of them—spent a whole night and all the next day guarding the empty train that we're going on, and fighting off a great mob of Poles who were trying to loot it. The Poles hardly managed to steal anything.

After the robbery our boys got some rifles and machine-guns, and all by themselves loaded eight carriages full of food and medicine and things from the Red Cross. The result was that they didn't get any sleep for two whole days and nights. When they finally reached us, by a special train, a terrible storm was raging.

Karel Kavan is such a gentleman. He brought some milk for Pepíček, and some dried onion flakes for me. And a Russian girl in the food-stall by the station canteen gave me a big handful of tea, while Vera got half a sweet bun—really thoughtful, generous presents.

I can't describe how lonely and miserable I feel. Only my faith in God and my strange belief that I am safe in His hands keeps me above water. . . . Otherwise I would sink into despair. Why didn't I believe in Him so strongly before? My faith is a great gift, a reward for all the suffering. Quite seriously, I think it makes it all worth it.

Today Karel Stern has been talking about my Uncle Franci. He says that my uncle behaved quite beautifully in Auschwitz, and he thinks that he left with Cousin Milan for some labour camp. So perhaps I shall see somebody from my family after all! But where is my Sasha—my dearest darling? Please God, watch over him and bring him back home to me safely. My beloved. My dearest.

We're on the move again. On our train are ten American pilots destined for Lwów. It's hard to believe that our journey will ever end.

The pilots look spotless; their leather belts and shoes are shining. They seem to look at us with distrust and disdain. Obviously they haven't the slightest idea who we are, and we are hardly going to tell them.

We've also got a sort of choir on board—if you can call them that. They're singing like devils, belting out a marching song—'Šly panenky silnicí'*—perhaps to try and make our train go a bit faster. It's painfully slow at the moment.

Anyway, I have to stop now. It's too dark to write any more.

21st March

The first day of spring. During the night it was so hot in our carriage that I slept naked.

For most of the time we've been standing still—I mean the train has been standing still. But this morning at last we reached Chyrów. People swarmed about our train, selling all manner of things: eggs, butter, milk, fruit, even a whole roast chicken for 50 roubles.

I have no money left, so my interest in all this was purely academic.

Most of the people in our carriage are Hungarian-speakers; if they try to speak Czech it sounds horrible. It grates on my ears—and the sound of the Hungarian language makes me uncomfortable too.

Today I lost my temper and hit poor Roza, just because she didn't hear what I was telling her! I feel as lost and miserable as I did when I was sixteen, when my mother died: but even then, my terrible sadness and longing were mingled with hope for the future.

When I close my eyes, and the train is rocking like a

*'Young girls marching on the road.'

cradle, I can sometimes believe that all the horrors never happened, that I am not a lonely and bedraggled 29-year-old woman with cropped hair, dressed in a stolen German dress several sizes too big for her and dirty linen trousers, but a rich young girl, drifting off to sleep in a *wagon-lit* which is whisking her off to Paris. And from Paris I am going to write to Sasha and to Father, to tell them I've arrived safely and that they're not to worry about me. . . . But as soon as I open my eyes I can see the prison rags on everyone around me, and the coarse voices of the Hungarians grate on my ears once again.

The first day of spring! The sun is shining. Perhaps God will look after me. I feel like a small child—helpless—only hoping. 'Qui vivra, verra. . . . Whoever lives will see.'

I've been asking a lot of people about Fricek Gratum, but nobody knows anything about him.

22nd March

I feel like a jug brimming over with tears—happy, bitter tears. The countryside is beautiful—gentle rolling hills—and we are only forty kilometres from the Czechoslovak border.

It's the most glorious early spring day. The snow-capped mountain-tops seem to be running alongside our train. Some of the girls are standing in the open doorways of the carriage and singing.

Many of us are weeping, or struggling to hold back the tears. This is our *home*! Our *country*! It's impossible to explain what these precious words mean to us.

Six years ago it was because I loved my country so much that I didn't want to emigrate. So perhaps I am to blame for everything, since it was me who prevented Sasha and Father from leaving too. Who knows? If we could turn back time, and cross this frontier together today, I would be the happiest person on earth. But even now, alone, I thank God for keeping me alive to see this moment.

23rd March

Our train—or at least a third of it—is standing amidst the snow-capped hills in the most wonderful countryside, bathed in sunlight. They are taking the carriages a few at a time over the highest of the Beskidy Mountains. Our frontier is only a kilometre from here.

Yesterday I was so disappointed when I was told that it would probably be night-time when we crossed the border. . . . But then the train stopped. When we were all feeling thoroughly depressed, we suddenly heard the strains of our national anthem. From somewhere we could hear the most beautiful, magical voices, singing with crystal clarity, and all sixty of the women in our carriage seemed simultaneously to hold their breath. It was as if our homeland was sending us a greeting in song.

At about 10 o'clock this morning a group of four gypsies came to play for everyone on the train. They played horribly out of tune, but the soldiers who were standing around gave them some money. One of the soldiers, whose name was Grištra, started to dance—as gracefully and beautifully as only a Russian can. Then the oldest of the gypsies came over to our carriage and whispered to one of my friends—the one we call 'Pirozhki'*—'Jews and gypsies? That's almost the same, isn't it!' This idea obviously gave him great pleasure.

In the morning we had a snowball fight: there was Kavan, and Fritsch, and Strass, but I couldn't think about anyone but my Sasha. It seems like only yesterday that we were throwing snowballs at each other in Potštejn, with the same sun shining on us. Jirka Kořátko, Maruška, Jirka Vyscočil and his Anka were all there—so silly and so happy!

I have a frightful cold just now, and I can't stop coughing. I've got terrible bronchitis. What's going to become of me?

26th March

I'm on the way to Košice. Vera is staying behind in Uzhhorod with her Uncle Schretter. She doesn't care about me any more, she feels safe with her uncle.

My darling Pepíček is in Uzhhorod too. He's being looked after by the family of a Rabbi who spent the war hiding in the mountains with a group of partisans. He is married, and he has two children already, but he insisted on taking Pepíček—unfortunately. I'm feeling wretched about it, but I know I was too weak to look after him myself.

Roza is going back to Mukachevo, and she's been trying to talk me into going with her. She is sitting next to me at

*'Pastries' (Russian).

this very moment. Perhaps I could go, just to be with someone.

I spent last night at the house of some strangers—a very kind couple, with six dark-eyed little children. Feldman not only took us there: he also brought us some food and apples and even some money. In the morning a friendly carter gave us a lift to the railway-station, so now we are sitting in a nice clean carriage, travelling like ladies.

Now it's half past twelve, and we're getting off the train again—I don't know where.

27th March

Nové Město. We have been here since yesterday. We didn't get any sleep last night—actually I think this is the second night that we've been without food or sleep.

Of the 760 people who set off with us from Częstochowa, only two hundred are left.

We have been exploring this charming little town with Mr Fuchs and Mr Fiala. It's very pretty and quite undamaged, and with its hills covered with vineyards it looks like a little piece of Italy.

Now at last we have found a train, but we are still looking for food. I'm feeling cheerful, despite the heat and the endless waiting at every point on the line.

31st March

We are riding through the town of Třebišov on the back of

an army lorry. The soldiers here gave us a wonderful welcome, showering us with food and offers of accommodation.

On to Košické Olšany, just outside Košice. In the spring sunshine, there's a real Easter atmosphere—with brightly painted eggs, and milk and cakes on display everywhere.

We've also been to look round Košice itself, and in the hospital we found one of Sasha's schoolfriends, little Jan Polák. He's now in charge of Dr Picha's children's clinic here. The hospital is full of 'our people'—doctors and nurses who have come here from England—and they seemed genuinely pleased to see us. We are definitely all moving to Košice today, which is good, because we'd already been told to leave the military quarters where we've been staying.

Honza Fischer is in Prešov. Meissner brought me greetings from Honza, and said that he may go to Košice too. Dr Kafka, who I met at the National Council, knew my father and mother. I've also met a kind nurse called Dita Schulmannová, who is the matron at the hospital.

We are staying at the Hotel Imperial. There are six of us now: Alice Morellová, Mr Fiala, Pohl, Dr Liebiger, Petr and me. Fuchs had to stay behind to look after our luggage at Fitsche's house. Yesterday Fitsche promised that he was going to be at home—but he wasn't.

We drove to Košice in a car. They were sweeping the road in front of us, either for us or for President Beneš, who is supposed to be arriving tomorrow. I hope it was for us!

The countryside is really spring-like, with catkins everywhere and small yellow flowers on the hillsides. Every so often we see abandoned trenches and old German helmets. The countryside is full of them.

Now Dr Kafka has just arrived.

1st April

Last night we had a nice social evening at the hospital. It went on until half past one in the morning, and afterwards I slept in a child's bed.

In the morning I happened to meet Stefa Petr Nejedlová, who I hadn't seen for ten years, and amazingly she recognised me. She told me that she spent the war in Moscow. Her husband Vitek died of typhus.

2nd April

Today at last I was reunited with Honza Fischer. He's put on weight so fast that he looks bloated: but under all that fat, it's the same old Honza I knew in the Terezín ghetto. On the surface he seems a bit rough, but it's clear that he really is fond of me, and I feel relaxed in his company.

It's a nice feeling—at last a human being I know. But in spite of this I still feel desolate, and my longing for Sasha is stronger than ever. I want my husband—not a friend, not a lover, nothing like that—just tranquillity, peace and genuine love. Take pity on me, Lord, and bring Sasha back to me . . . I beg you!

3rd April

Today President Beneš arrived in Košice from England. A huge reception had been organised for him in front of the theatre. Mr Fiala persuaded me to stay there with him and listen for four whole hours 'to witness history in the making', which I've now discovered is extremely boring.

In the evening I had a long discussion with Honza as we walked together in the park. He's not planning to stay here for long.

I've been given a lovely little room in the Green Cross Hotel. It's the first time in six years that I've had a room to myself.

13th April

I have a job! I am now a civil servant at the Ministry of Information. The minister's name is Kopecký. My salary is 3000 Czech crowns a month, and I've already spent half of it.

27th April

Yesterday evening the Russian army occupied Brno. The Americans have occupied Cheb, and the Russians have entered Bremen and Stettin.

There is barely anything left of the old Germany. Berlin is surrounded.

There has been an uprising in northern Italy. Partisans have taken Genoa, Milan and the whole of the north.

Göring has resigned.

The Russian and American armies are expected to meet up today.

Alice Morellová has left for Trebišov to manage the local hospital there. Honza has joined the Free Czech Army. He's been broadcasting to Prague with Pat'a and me.

Prague is still in German hands, and there are rumours that

the Germans have set Prague Castle on fire—God forbid.

28th April

Munich has been taken.

29th April

Himmler has offered to capitulate, but only to the USA and Britain. Mussolini has been executed by Italian partisans.

30th April

A group of Czech fascists are saying that the Germans should be allowed to leave Prague and go freely to Bavaria. General Klecanda is expected to be put in charge until the Russians and British arrive. The workers in the Skoda arms factories are on strike.

1st May

May Day celebrations. The folk costumes are beautiful and the weather is perfect.

I have jaundice and look very yellow. . . . And I've been crying. Somebody told me that Gustav Schorsch is dead— apparently he couldn't take the hard labour in the mines or the brutal treatment from the Schupos. Also that the SS shot Gideon Klein and Rafik Schachtr, after first setting fire to the prisoners' barracks.

In the afternoon I went for a walk with Gustav Solar. We went up the hill at Calvary and found a wooden Russian statue of Christ, beautifully carved and with a wonderfully strong expression. A Russian general brought it here a few days ago.

Then I had a nice talk with Gusta on Cistorin Hill. We talked until half past seven in the evening. Afterwards we were bored stiff by a variety show at the local theatre.

For the last two nights I've had the most vivid dreams about Sasha. In one dream he was saved, but in last night's dream when he returned he was insane and didn't want to stay with me. When he left I knew that he wanted to kill himself.

I don't know how long I can endure this uncertainty. Sometimes I feel that I'm going mad myself. I can't stand it.

About a week ago I met Franta Fleischmann, my mother's cousin. He's just arrived from England, fat and stupid. He told me that he is now a big-shot at the Finance Ministry. He gave me all sorts of presents.

He is kind—but stupid.

1st May, 10 p.m.

Hitler has fallen. I've just heard the announcement on German radio.

9th May

At midnight on the night of the 8th and 9th of May, Germany's unconditional surrender was ratified in Berlin.

At last there is peace.

30th May

Today I got a message from Jirka Wachtl. My Sasha died on the 20th of April 1945 in a village called Kraslice, near Carlsbad.

He died on an open wagon, surrounded by twenty-one dead and dying girls who had been brought from Buchenwald.

Wachtl was there: he managed to escape from the cart, with his brother Ota and their father, so he knows what happened.

I just had to go to Kraslice. Gusta Bareš drove me there, passing through Kutná Hora on the way.

I have now turned a dark yellow colour. A doctor has told me that I may be dying. So what?

Sasha is buried somewhere in a heap of ashes near the railway-station here. He is lying in a mass grave.

Now is the end of happiness. Of love. Of hope. The end of my naive prayers. The end of my youth. The end, when it should have been a beginning. All that is left is a miserable half-existence.

I was writing this diary for you, Sasha.

For you I could endure the hunger and the cold. For you I could reach the end of the road. I didn't want to die. But without you, my life is meaningless. It's so hard to live even from one minute to the next.

Dear heart, I don't know how much longer I can go on. But perhaps we shall see each other again. I know I'll die, and I hope it'll be soon.

20th November

I am in Prague. It's eight years since you kissed me for the first time, Sasha.

After my show tonight we went to the U Šupů Restaurant, but it was all closed up, and inside it was completely dark.

Now I am sitting in our favourite coffeehouse, the Union, at our table in the middle room. I'm warming my hands on a cup of tea, just as I used to in the old days. The street hasn't changed at all. You're sitting opposite me. Your mother has just left us. You're the only person for me in the whole world. . . . The only one.

The world is empty and I can't stand it. I want to die.

If only I had some poison. . . . The idea of jumping out of a window terrifies me. It's so disgustingly messy. I suppose one doesn't know until the last moment whether one is really going to do it. Perhaps I shouldn't be so ashamed of not being able to decide.

Sasha, you have gone there before me—like Father, and Jirka Platovský, and Fricek, and Aunt Olga—Aunt Roza—Uncle Ota—Uncle Franci—Jirka Pick—Jozina Neumannová and Maminka. Are you waiting for me there?

It would be so much easier if you could give me a sign, anything, to let me know. Why don't you try it, Sasha?

I would do anything to be with you again. I would even join the transport from Terezín to Auschwitz again.

Wherever I go, I just long to be with you. . . . It doesn't matter where. And yet at the same time I find myself suddenly thinking about the future, about getting married again and having children—mad, illogical thoughts, like broken snatches of tunes which swirl around one's head with no recognisable melody.

My dearest. My beloved. Ask God to forgive me. Pray for my soul—the soul I am losing. I don't want to live with a shattered soul.

Please help me to die.

And yet—I know I have to go through it alone. I fought death so strongly when it was so close, and so maybe it's what I deserve.

Goodbye, my dear golden Milan, and forgive me. You have outlived your mother, and your brother, and you will outlive me as well.

Anežka—thank you, and look after my dog Susanna.

Honza—goodbye. Don't kill yourself too. You are younger than me, and your situation isn't the same.

Milan, if you can, give some of my money to our theatre. And give a ring or some other trinket to Anežka. Give something to Karla Nauková too.

Take my ashes to Kraslice. To Sasha. I would like to be near him, even if it means being surrounded by the bodies of so many unknown girls. We belong to them. And give something to Maruška Kořátková too.

And now I'm going to try and do it. I'm frightened. . . . But perhaps I'll succeed?

Epilogue

4th January 1996

No, I did not succeed in killing myself.

My shabby and barely legible diary reached me a few days before Christmas 1995. Where did I get the blank notebook from? Perhaps I found it in one of the deserted houses in Poland or Silesia.

It was sent to me from Australia by my old Czech friend Lola Schott. It must have been hiding in some old suitcase or other for fifty whole years! But why has she only just found it? And why has she sent it to me without a word of explanation?

There are so many little details, so many names I had almost forgotten. Everything came back to me. But there are also many gaps in the diary, things I remember vividly but which I left out. Perhaps I felt that they were not so important for me then—not worth writing about.

I will end this epilogue quickly. Between 1945 and 1948 I was a member of the Realistic Theatre Company in Prague.

Acting—even bad acting—was good for me, much better than an asylum. In the theatre I met my second husband, Jirka Pravda, the best actor and the kindest man in the world, full of love and understanding; he saved my life. I wanted a child, and we had a baby—a son. We called him Sasha.

My dearest Jirka died after thirty-nine years of wonderful marriage, on the 1st of May 1985. He was sixty-eight years old. Jirka always knew that Sasha Munk was my first and deepest love. My son now has four beautiful children, and he is good to me.

I didn't speak to Pat'a or Honza or the others about Auschwitz, the gas chambers and the unending horror, because we all went through it. This is the diary of an escapee—the diary of a free person.

There are plenty of books about the concentration camps, all similar to each other, all horrifying, and different only in the reactions of each personality who lived through them. My diary was completely private—not written as an accusation, or as the memoirs of a witness. And it was written then.

I can't forgive the perpetrators of this evil, nor do I want to forgive. I have never obtained a mandate from all the innocent victims to do so. I want to remember the victims always, and I believe that the guilty should be punished.

But there is some hope in my heart. Vaguely, childishly, I still believe in God and in immortality, and that gives me the strength to go on living, as I hope it does for others as well.

HANA PRAVDA (HANA MUNK), NÉE HANA BECK

Sasha Munk
13th February 1914–20th April 1945

'Dear Hana . . .'

Melbourne, 5th February 1996

Dear Hana,

Today I am going to write to you again, to make up for the letter that I wrote before Christmas and which was obviously lost in the Christmas mail.

Antony's opinion was that I should not send you your war diary because it would bring back painful memories and make you miserable. I thought completely the opposite, and from your reaction in your recent letter, I was right.

I'll tell you how I found the diary. When we were in Paris in 1948–49, just after we'd emigrated, my brother-in-law Josef (who went to school with your cousin Milan) was working at the American Institute in Prague, and he was able to meet quite a lot of American tourists. If he discovered that they were travelling back through Paris, he used to ask them to take us parcels of some of the books we'd been forced to leave behind in Prague.

One day, among the parcels, there was something which one of my relatives had given me many years beforehand: a black lacquered and silver-trimmed jewel-case, about 20 centimetres long, 18 centimetres wide and 7 centimetres deep. Inside were some gloves and handkerchiefs, and to be honest I was rather surprised. I couldn't understand why Josef had sent it. So I put it with the rest of our luggage and forgot all about it. I had plenty of things to worry about besides gloves in those days!

I remember giving you and Jirka some of the Czech books, but of course I never thought of mentioning the old lacquered box.

Still, when we followed you to Melbourne, we took the box with us. As you know, we stayed for almost a year in your house there, and then moved first to Rosebery Street and eventually to Cole Street in East Hawthorn.

Quite recently I was looking for a little gift for a friend, and I took that old box out of my wardrobe again. The gloves were no longer there: and then, I don't know why, I suddenly noticed a small ribbon sticking out from the black velvet lining at the bottom of the box. I pulled the ribbon, and the false bottom lifted up. Incidentally, the false bottom was a bit larger than the box and had been folded round the edges, so no one could have guessed that anything was hidden under it. . . . But there was your little red diary.

When I picked it up, the photograph of your husband Sasha Munk fell out. I recognised him immediately, and suddenly realised that the little book must be yours. So I closed it again at once. I didn't know until I received your letter that a lock of your mother's hair was in it as well.

I have no further explanation about all this, and it's too late now to ask my brother-in-law because he died about six years ago. It remains a mystery to me why he took so much trouble to hide your diary—although we have to remember what it was like in the days of the Communist police state.

Today in Melbourne it's 30 degrees in the shade. I'm writing with the windows closed and the Venetian blinds drawn. . . . I hate the heat and will never get used to it. I can't wait for autumn, just as you probably can't wait for spring.

Do you have any photos from your family get-together last Christmas? Please send us some—as soon as possible!

Lots of love,

Lola

Biographical notes

Hana Pravda lost not just her husband in the Holocaust, but also her father, her paternal grandmother, her Aunt Olga and Uncle Ota, her Aunt Roza, and her Uncle Franci together with his two children Jarka and Jiří Stein. Her beloved cousin Jirka Platovský was beaten to death at a labour camp in Kladno in 1944, when the Gestapo discovered that he had a non-Jewish girlfriend; they had found a letter from her hidden in one of his shoes.

Among Hana Pravda's friends mentioned in the diary, victims included Jirka Pick, who had had polio as a child but who showed remarkable courage in the Terezín ghetto; the theatre director Gustav Schorsch; the musician Rafík Schachtr, who had famously conducted a performance of Smetana's *The Bartered Bride* in the Terezín ghetto; and her husband's closest friend from his schooldays, Fricek Gratum, who was shot by SS men after trying to escape from a transport on the way to Bergen-Belsen.

One of the only members of her family to survive was Milan Platovský ('cousin Milan'). In the last months of the War, while being transported from Auschwitz to Sachsenhausen in an open railway-wagon, he was so enraged to see an SS man kicking a dying prisoner that he hurled him out of the carriage and killed him. The other SS man in the carriage promptly befriended him

The Stein children.
Clockwise, from top left:
Roza, Franci, Olga, and
Beatrix (Hana's mother).
Roza and Olga were to
die at Auschwitz, Franci
at a labour camp near
Hamburg.

and saved him from being punished. Soon after reaching
Sachsenhausen the guards fled, and the prisoners found
themselves on their own. Milan Platovský was one of the few
strong enough to go looking for food: and on finding a sack of
potatoes he managed to carry it back to his fellow prisoners, who
happened to include a 61-year-old former political activist named
Antonín Zápotocký. After the War, when Zápotocký became
prime minister of the Czechoslovak Republic, he repaid Milan
Platovský's kindness by granting him a visa to leave the country.
Milan emigrated to Chile, where he set up a successful
import–export business. In 1999 he was honoured by the Czech

government for services to the Czech economy, and in the same year he published his autobiography *Přežít a Žít* (*Survive and Live*).

Vera Kornová, who also lost almost her entire family in the War, subsequently moved to Prague before emigrating to Montreal in the 1950s. She married a man named Sasha Bondi and had twin boys. She was joined in Canada by her Uncle Schretter (see entry for 26th March), who had served with the Allies during the War.

Karel Kavan and Honza Fischer, who had been members of the amateur dramatic group in the Terezín ghetto (see pages 20–1), both settled in Prague after the War. Honza Fischer, who had been strongly influenced by Hana Pravda, embarked on a career at the Czech National Theatre, eventually becoming director.

Jirka Strass and Jirka Vyskočil also pursued careers in the theatre, and later helped to establish the highly influential Black Theatre Company (in which actors, wearing black and with only their hands and faces illuminated, perform against a black background).

Paťa Fischl emigrated to Israel in 1948, and devoted

Milan Platovský and his wife Jana.

Jirka Platovský.

considerable efforts to collecting eye-witness accounts from survivors of the Holocaust. He also encouraged Hana Pravda to leave Czechoslovakia: and in 1985 she visited him and his American wife Betty at their home in Tel Aviv.

Jirka Kořátko also survived the War and acted as witness at Hana Pravda's second marriage. The organisers of the wedding reception—mistaking him for a prominent government minister of the same name—surprised everyone by providing large quantities of free food.

Dita Schulmannová, who had spent most of the War working as a doctor in London, later settled permanently in England, becoming Hana's closest friend after the Pravdas arrived in London in 1956.

Stefa Petr Nejedlová did not keep in contact with Hana Pravda after the War. Her father-in-law, the writer and historian Zdeněk

One of the first things Hana Munk did after returning to Prague in 1945 was to erect a memorial by her mother's grave. The inscription reads: 'These are the members of my family murdered in concentration camps by the Nazis during the 1939–45 War.'

Nejedlý (whom Hana remembers as 'smarmy and lecherous'), later collaborated with Stalin and went on to become minister of culture in the Czechoslovak Republic.

Sasha Munk's friend Jirka Wachtl emigrated to Sydney after the War.

Gusta Bareš became editor of the extreme Communist

newspaper *Rudé Právo*. He was later imprisoned by the Communist authorities following a show trial.

The Hungarian kapo and her twelve-year-old daughter survived the death march from Birnbäumel and their subsequent imprisonment at Bergen-Belsen, which was to have been Hana Pravda's destination too.

Gideon Klein, the brilliant pianist and composer (and protégé of Josef Beck's), did not survive the War: in November 1944 he was sent to Auschwitz, and from there to Fürstengrube in Silesia, where he died at the age of twenty-six. After the War, however, his compositions were rescued from their hiding-place in Terezín by his sister Elizabeth Kleinová, who championed them and ensured their subsequent popularity.

Of Pepíček, Hana Pravda writes: 'I don't remember where we found him, but he was a little Czech boy, just five years old in 1945. He was one of the twins who the satanic Dr Mengele saved from the gas chambers to conduct his experiments on. Pepíček spoke about his twin sister, but couldn't remember how he had lost her. He told us how the little children in his barracks used to help each other to get dressed every morning. His memories of the SS men and the Schupos had got completely mixed up with Grimm's fairy-tales, so that one moment he would be speaking about some Schupo women, and the next moment about the witch in a fairy-tale. He couldn't distinguish between them at all.'

To her lasting regret, Hana Pravda never discovered what became of Pepíček after the War.

Chronology

Winter 1914	Marriage of Josef Beck and Beatrix Stein in Prague
Spring 1917	*Tomáš Masaryk forms Czechoslovak Legion among ex-prisoners of war in Russia*
Oct 1918	*Czechoslovakia proclaimed an independent republic under Tomáš Masaryk*
— 1921	Dr Josef Beck, Hana's father, returns from service with the Czechoslovak Legion
18 June 1932	Beatrix Beck, Hana's mother ('Maminka'), dies of leukaemia
30 Jan 1933	*Hitler appointed chancellor of Germany*
Summer 1933	Hana Beck appears in her first film, *Marijka Nevěrnice* (*Marijka the Unfaithful*)
Dec 1935	*Masaryk resigns presidency in favour of his foreign minister Eduard Beneš*
— 1936	Hana Beck meets Sasha Munk at a political meeting

1936–37	Hana Beck attends drama school in Leningrad under Alexei Dikii
28–30 Sept 1938	*British, French and Italian leaders (Chamberlain, Daladier and Mussolini) support Hitler's claims to the Sudeten region of Czechoslovakia at Munich Conference*
Oct 1938	*German troops enter Sudetenland; President Beneš goes into exile in England*
15 Mar 1939	*Hitler invades Czechoslovakia*
27 Apr 1939	Hana Beck marries Sasha Munk
3 Sept 1939	*Britain and France declare war on Germany*
Autumn 1939	Hana and Sasha Munk move to Potštejn in the Czech countryside
31 May 1942	*Gestapo leader Reinhard Heydrich dies following ambush by Czech patriots*
Dec 1942	Hana and Sasha Munk transported to Terezín ghetto
1 Oct 1944	Hana and Sasha Munk transported to Auschwitz
Oct 1944	Hana Munk transported to labour camp at Birnbäumel
12–17 Jan 1945	*Soviets launch massive offensive from Polish bridgeheads of Magnuszów, Pulawy and Sandomierz, and enter Częstochowa*
21 Jan 1945	Death march sets off from Birnbäumel to Bergen-Belsen
27 Jan 1945	*Auschwitz liberated*

29 Jan 1945	Hana Munk escapes from death march
3 Feb 1945	*Soviets establish bridgeheads across the Odra, 40 miles from Berlin*
23 Mar 1945	Hana Munk returns to Czechoslovakia
3 Apr 1945	*Eduard Beneš returns from exile and forms a national government in Košice*
20 Apr 1945	Sasha Munk dies at Kraslice, western Czechoslovakia
30 Apr 1945	*Hitler commits suicide*
8 May 1945	*German surrender ratified in Berlin.*

Editor's note

On first reading Hana Pravda's translation of her diary, and the epilogue she had prepared for a BBC World Service broadcast, I was intrigued particularly by her statement that 'there are many gaps in the diary, things I remember vividly but which I left out'. At that time I was unaware that in transcribing the diary she had already added some of these memories, in order to clarify certain parts of the story.

When I subsequently noticed discrepancies between the transcript and the manuscript diary (now deposited at the Imperial War Museum, London), I initially felt that the integrity of the original document had been compromised, and that I ought to print only what had actually been written in 1945. Mrs Pravda felt differently. The original diary did not tell the full story, she argued, and since all the memories were genuine, what did it matter that some of them had not been recorded on paper at the time?

The fact is that all diaries are written after the events they describe. The interval may be only a few moments or hours, but on occasions it may be years (as in the case of Michihiko Hachiya's *Hiroshima Diary*, written up from sketchy notes kept after the dropping of the first atomic bomb) or even decades (as with parts of the diary of Samuel Pepys's great contemporary, John Evelyn).

The current edition, therefore, may be seen as containing two diaries, which together not only tell a remarkable story: they also shed light on the very nature of human memory, and the way that apparently trivial details often stick in the mind far longer than those which may at first seem important. Hana Pravda maintains that the two diaries are inseparable; but, for the record, the 'second diary' consists of the following passages:

21–26.1: paragraph (pg) 5, sentence (s) 3. 27.1: pg 3, s 4–pg 4. 29.1: pg 16, s 2–3; pg 21; pg 32; pg 38, s 3; pg 42–44. 30.1: pg 1. 8.2: pg 2; pg 6–7. 9–12.2: pg 1, s 3, 5; pg 3–4; pg 5, s 2–pg 6, s 1; pg 6, s 3; pg 6, s 5–pg 7; pg 8, s 2; pg 10, s 3–pg 11. 13.2: pg 1; pg 5, s 3–pg 6. 14.2–7.3: pg 2, s 2–pg 3, s 1; pg 4, s 3–4; pg 9–14; pg 17–18. 10.3: pg 2–14, s 2. 16.3: pg 3, s 1–4, 6, 7. 19.3: pg 13, s 3–pg 14. 26.3: pg 2. 31.3: pg 4, s 4. 27.4: pg 6, s 3–pg 7. 30.5: pg 1, s 1; pg 3; pg 4, s 2–pg 6.

List of illustrations

Further reading

Martin Gilbert, *The Holocaust: The Jewish Tragedy*. London: Harper Collins, 1986.

Martin Gilbert, *Atlas of the Holocaust*, revised edn. London: Routledge, 1994.

Martin Gilbert, *Holocaust Journey*. London: Weidenfeld & Nicolson, 1997.

Daniel Jonah Goldhagen, *Hitler's Willing Executioners*. London: Little, Brown, 1996.

Gerald Green, *The Artists of Terezín*. New York: Schocken, 1978.

Raul Hilberg, *Perpetrators, Victims, Bystanders: The Jewish Catastrophe*. London: Lime Tree, 1993.

Callum MacDonald & Jan Kaplan, *Prague in the Shadow of the Swastika: A History of the German Occupation 1939–1945*. London: Quartet, 1995.